In Hardy Country

In Hardy Country

New and Selected Poems
by
Tom Dawe

BREAKWATER

Breakwater
100 Water Street
P.O. Box 2188
St. John's, NF
A1C 6E6

*Cover Painting: "House Where Nobody Lives" by
Gerry Squires (from the M.U.N. collection)*

Canadian Cataloguing in Publication Data
   Dawe, Tom.

      In hardy country

      Poems.
      ISBN 1-55081-056-1

   I. Title.

PS8557.A847I64 1993   C811'.54   C92-098682-X
PR9199.3.D33I64   1993

Acknowledgements

Some of these poems (or versions of them) have appeared in earlier volumes:

Hemlock Cove and After (Breakwater)
Island Spell (Cuff)
In A Small Cove (Wychwood Press, U.K.)

Others have appeared in the following magazines and anthologies:

The Atlantic Advocate
Baffles of Wind and Tide
Banked Fires
Choice Atlantic
CV-II
East of Canada
Easterly
The Fiddlehead
Landings
The Newfoundland Quarterly
31 Newfoundland Poets
Other Voices
Poet (India)
The Pottersfield Portfolio
Riverine (Ireland)
Stages
Themes For All Times
Tickle Ace

Some other books by Tom Dawe:

(Poetry)
Hemlock Cove and After
Island Spell
In a Small Cove

(Folklore)
The Loon In The Dark Tide:
Old Newfoundland Ghost Stories
The Yarns of Ishmael Drake

(Children's)
Landwash Days
A Gommil From Bumblebee Bight
Lings N' Things
Angishore, Boo-man and Clumper
Alley-coosh, Bibby and Cark
Winter Of The Black Weasel

With love
to my mother,
Marjorie Dawe,
prime among those
who never let me forget
that best
and worst
of places,
my own hardy country.

Contents

In Hardy Country

For me, it's no county overseas,
        no Avon, Berkshire, Dorset,
        no Hampshire, Wiltshire, Somerset,
        no ancient temples, no mounds anymore,
        no West Country nappe all manicured now
        for a museum trade,
        no classical Max Gate drawing-room
        where Florence died.

For me, it's those drawn outport figures
        in Bonfire Night,
        the nip of a north wind and mummers'
        accordions rising on a moon...
        As the fire expires,
        the stranger in the kitchen
        is spinning a story
        about one of the last criminals
        to be hanged
        out through a courthouse window
        for a crowd on Water Street...

        It's my mother too and the way
        that she looked at me once,
        so wistfully,
        in wood-stove light,
        recalling her young womanhood
        in a Canadian Depression,
        and the wonderful man
        she was going to marry
        in Montreal before any rumours of war,
        or just some small coincidence,
        perhaps,
        in that far summer
        on St. Catherine's Street,
        made her return,
        regretfully,
        to Newfoundland.

A Fairy Tale

My great grandmother
is a young girl
lost in the woods.
She carries a berry bucket
and cries
because she has no money
to drive the fairies away.

Watching her,
I am old enough
to be her father.

Her path sinks deeper
into red turf
and bright leaves are sharp.
Old wood has reaching arms
and grey, knobby legs.
Branches are glowing fingers
that cup and cradle the sun.
Faintly, she hears music
on a soft, sap breath
and knows it is not the brook.
Far far away are calling boys
with jam stains on their lips
and laughing girls
clumsy in black, rubber boots
and a clang of dippers.

Just before twilight
she walks out of the woods
and finds a young man fencing
near a crab-apple tree.
He runs to his father
for a horse and cart
and offers her
a ride back home.

On the long way back
through lingering,
still-twig light
they sit close together.
He hums an old love song
learned by some fireside.
The grass is long and green
right up the middle of the road.
Between her knees

she holds her day's berries
like a cask of jewels.

I am patiently waiting
to be born
and wondering
when the cart
will turn into a turnip
or a big red apple on wheels.

I call out to them
as they slide down
gradually
into leafy sunset.
Waving my empty dipper
I run after them.
But they ignore me.
The night closes
around everything.
And strange stars
come out.

Riddle

I see them in summer
twilight,
six or seven sitting in a kitchen.
The lights are not on yet
and my father comes
in through the door
from the day's cod-splitting.
Behind him the horns of a new moon
rise up from a cloud bank.
The tide is pulsing
up the ladders of a stage head.
Cleansed by an afternoon
of blood
and salt-spilling,
father is straight and tall,
joking as he takes the beams
on his shoulders
and joins the others
in a riddle spell.

Patient as anchor rust,
he awaits his turn
before he offers:
"What goes over the water,
and under the water,
without touching the water?"
In the pause,
the sea whispers.
Then grandfather answers:
"An egg in a duck's belly."

My mother,
six weeks married,
smiles coyly
in a corner.
Much against their wishes,
she has been swimming
all by herself
again this afternoon
over on Swan Island.
She has not told anybody yet
that she is expecting me.

Still Life

From the fall of the wind:
a cap full of crab apples
brought to a kitchen table
by my nine-year-old sister
from a garden
near a beach wall.

(Somewhere in pock-marked light,
my mother is weeping.
That cap, tossed from a train
one Sunday afternoon,
has reminded her again
of my brother
who is seventeen
and somewhere
on the mainland.)

By those bitter apples:
two baccalieu birds
bleeding
near a china bowl.
(Father, in a shadow
near a gun-rack,
is always returning
from another day
on the water.)

(Grandmother, old pious penguin
with her apron on,
waddles down
from her picture frame.
With a sweep of her arm,
she scatters my paper and crayons,
telling me to go
and do something useful
for a change.)

Devil At The Dance

Somewhere in the lore of long ago
In the place where I come from,
A stranger appeared at a dance one night
As a man of music and song.

The young and old revolved in his reel,
He fiddled the stars from the sky;
The Devil assumed such a pleasing shape
As the time went spinning by.

But just on the verge of cautious dawn,
Someone spied his cloven foot,
So he disappeared in a brimstone cloud
And a drizzling rain of soot.

There's not one trace of that floor today
Where weeds grow lush and long,
But people all along the coast
Still wonder if the dance goes on.

The Bogey Man

He was always
somewhere
in my bedtime dread
in the looming shadows
when mother threatened
to put the light out
if I didn't get to sleep.
Famished for child-flesh
he waited in a moth-ball cave
behind coat-hangers.
And on that first day
when mother released my hand
in the windy school yard
he assumed the form of a bully
watching me from the bridge.
Later, in the long lane
back from the store at night
when I was afraid
to look behind
he was footstep-echo
and whispering breath
on the back of my neck.
And there were places
along the coast
where he appeared
as the Black Doryman
or some questing devil
in a ghost skiff
roaming the waves
in the ungodly hours
to snatch any youngsters
straying on the beach.
In talk of war time
he was a foreign sailor
spying on us from a fog
or an American from a base
coming to carry girls away.
One day we were alerted
about a strange character
near the edge of the woods.
I could see his wolfish eyes
peering from dark boughs
when my aunt warned us
that he might even be
a Canadian
or something...

Solstice, Outport Childhood

deep snowfall
    still
        black hole
    of tadpole pool

hands around tea-mug
    an uncle
        remembering
    winters
in the lumberwoods

grandmother
    spinning
        daydreaming
her own version
    of rumpelstiltskin

cleaned for christmas
china
    along aunt clara's dresser
        light
from the sea

Uncle

Soap-scented, shiny by the lamp,
You looked down from your chair,
My brother's nose was dark with blood,
His knuckles bruised my ear.

You'd give the winner fifty cents,
You swore aloud by heaven;
My stocky brother was almost eight
And I was a skinny seven.

In a kitchen with the fire out,
We fought a savage round;
Father and Mother were gone that night
On a Saturday trip to town.

Outside, a devilish wind drove by
And rattled from eaves to floor;
We knocked some dishes from the shelf;
Your rum breath called for more.

You laughed and said we fought like men;
Your frolic cast a gleam;
You clutched that silver in your fist
The night you turned fifteen.

Peppermint Rock

If somebody asked me
for my earliest memory,
it would have to be
that day in Avalon
when I, just a drooling toddler,
dropped a great peppermint knob
into my infant brother's mouth.
There in the crib cage,
below a framed picture
of somebody's guardian angel,
he was kicking and crying,
a gaping hole of a mouth,
one chasm of grief
through which my world
was tumbling.
To appease the spirit
of this pit,
I rolled one of my precious
candy boulders
to the brink of the lip
and let it slip...

Here everything goes mad:
the baby, blue-black
swirls upside down
and mother
is slapping his back.
She is shouting at me.
I scurry under a table,
her wrath like a dogfish
after me.

I wait for that worst
which always happens.
Up in the glassy pictures
the ancestors all frown down.
Queen Victoria grows
another layer on her chin.
The guardian angel goes
for his or her sword...
The candy,
a slimy shiny ball,
chuckles on the floor...

I can laugh at it now,
the way I tried
to stuff his face that day.
It is only in my moralizing
moments
or bouts of self-pity
that I want to change this poem
and call it my earliest lesson:
how a gesture of pure
unadulterated generosity
can be so misunderstood,
or an act of kindness
can sometimes kill.

One Fall Night

Back in that forever
of growing-up to touch the sky,
back in those after-supper times,
there were long fall nights
when a full moon seemed to pull
on the stalks of the fields
and the old grey picket-fences
keeping all within bounds.
And there were a few big houses
stretching stories into a sky
that we could never reach.
One night we crept away
from those houses on the skyline,
from their frames of kitchen light
across a light frost marsh
down to the river that ignored
all lines of field and fence
as it let in the rising tide.
And big silver sea trout came in
on the pull of the new moon.
We heard them splashing
in the water below the fences
where we sat quietly,
so high on the top rails,
on the skyline now
with the houses we had left.

Outport Christmas

Once a year, at least
my mind becomes lined
with yellow paper
from old attic trunks
where sea-gulls glide
in a scent of apples;
cold turkeys recline
on china slabs
in delicious death
as I carry yet
the weight
of a pregnant woolen sock.
I stare through frost glass
holding up a cross;
I watch strange humps of rock
on the eastern snow.
The sock gives birth:
exotic candies
little shepherds
plastic fishes
on an icy morning floor.
I stand
holding the empty skin
under the darkness
of a dead tree
nailed to the roof
yesterday.

On Small Island

on path moss
        up from landwash
leaf sounds

in from sea
        cat paws
through long grass

bisecting pool
        and sky
the muskrat's wake

raindrops
        rock reflections
in lily pads

from grass spear
        sun drops
into pitcher plant

Boatman

I was taking my time,
sculling her back
from her husband's funeral
on that abandoned island
where he had asked
to be buried
with his ancestors.
She sat in the prow,
stiff as a figurehead,
watching the others
row on ahead.
Being just a boy
of twelve or so,
and free from school that day,
I thought her ancient
as the Old Hag of Nightmare,
but, looking back on it now,
she might have been
thirty or so,
all sad and lovely
in September sunshine.
With time on my side,
as I thought then,
I coasted,
letting the others leave us.
She never said a word,
even when I stopped
to watch mackerel spray
westward up the bay,
and sea trout swirl
near a river mouth.
Soon, all around us,
the sea was looking glass,
our cove a bowl of silver.
But when we reached shore,
she spoiled it all
when I heard her say
to a man on the wharf:
"What I'd like now
is a nice bit of salt fish."
And all I could think about

was her own poor man
alone forever
on that island
where loons bawled
in the evening time.

I thought she was callous,
cold, indifferent then,
but perhaps I was
much too literal-minded that day,
hardly the boatman
for the journey
she was taking.

Caretaker

I've heard it all before
from this wizened fellow
who comes each summer to tidy up
the old Methodist cemetery.
Today, an aged Tom Sawyer
without the apple,
with time on his hands,
he wants to regale me
with talk about the good old days.
He's fondling those markers again,
re-tracing the lettering,
stroking lambs, handshakes, harps
and cold angels carved on the tops.
He's stressing the warning
in every epitaph,
a fateful anecdote for each:

Once again the grim plight
of Poor Isaac
falling on his gun
in far beaver-country,
and young Richard cutting his foot
long before any miracle drugs
were around to save him;
and the legend of Oliver Brown
struck down by lightning,
and poor infant Sally,
forty years or so dead
from strawberries out of season,
resting there with her mother
who was nineteen herself
when she died.
He steps gingerly over a family
all victims of Spanish Flu
and whooping cough...

Soon he will switch the subject
to nuclear war,

the Bible
and the Middle East.
I wrestle with a weed-locked gate.
Any second now,
he'll be in ecstasy again
proclaiming no peace for our time,
pronouncing
that the world has come
a long way
from the safe
and steady place
it used to be.

A Day In '45

I lived as a child then
part property of girl-aunts
and grandparents
in old parlour pictures
that moved
in growing up
in sticks of grass
around large thickly-painted doors.
Somebody talked of "mushroom clouds"
and I looked up into a cloudless sky.
There was a hanging smell of gun-powder
around old muzzle-loaders
but only in a dusk-dark hall
of boots and coats.
And there were long cartridges
in back-room boxes with rabbit snares
and powder-horns and fishing poles.
Down beyond the house
my puddle was calm, mirror clean.
Not a ripple stirred the lily-pads
on a day when a rock was dropped
from the sun
into a distant sea.

The Dead Boy
(circa 1946)

Coppers on his eyes,
A new king's head right and left,
And sisters crying.

Coppers on his eyes
And grandmothers telling us
Of clear, golden streets.

Coppers on his eyes
And someone lifting us up
To see their shining.

Coppers on his eyes,
Enough for two candy canes,
But shop blinds are down.

Summerplace

aspen
        pane-tapping
tap dance
    in the dark

    rain roar
the peak of my grandfather's roof
      parting
             the sky

in lightning
         flash
            ancestors
       sepia
          frowns

Abandoned Outport

Sun on boarded windows
and gull cries
high in August clouds.

On a small beach-path:
blue-bells nodding
over driftwood.

A bee is buzzing
inside dark cracks
in a window pane.

Clover meadow:
above the rusting ploughshare
a butterfly.

A sudden fog
and sea-winds
bend the sting-nettle.

Deep in graveyard grass
snails and lichens
cling to the headstone.

Across the schoolhouse floor:
paper scraps, dry sea-weed
and a dead moth.

Against the cold twilight:
dark picket-fences
and a crow's flight.

In a rising moon:
a church steeple
and lilac leaves.

At Western Arm

There was once a saw-mill here
giving a swift brook
its last fling
before it found the sea again.
There were houses too
with small front gardens
where lilacs shook
in fiord winds
and somebody turned earth
to plant an apple
or a rose tree
or some spot
of bleeding hearts.
Between the gardens
there were snaking
narrow lanes
where sweating horses toiled
between mist of dawn
and lantern light.

Now everything is gone
down
in a tangle
of alders
and the slow
revenge
of the birch.

Dark Morning

A phantom ship drifts by
The yawning cove;
Cold kettles are anchored
On cast-iron stoves;

Damp dories bob
In metal north-eastern light;
The beach holds perished caplin
Of last night.

There's not one upstairs scuff
Of woolen sock;
A short hand points to four
On a rusty clock.

The Mummer

I was once the best mummer
in our cove.
I pleased the people
all the time.
And through the Christmas spell
I mummered by myself
across drifted fields
and tricky paths
above the cliffs
on raw nights
when sea voices whispered
in caves far below me.
I clutched my kerosene lantern
and felt my old accordion
wheeze against my ribs.
And in all those winter times
with my light coming to hers,
she always let me in,
though she never guessed me
and I did not lift my veil.
Not once did she guess
that all those tunes I played
of long-gone summer love
and never-forgetting
were just for her.
Though they danced and laughed
and shook the china on the shelves,
her youngsters could never know
how I played for mother alone.
Though they shone
with cake crumbs and syrup
on their happy faces,
I never played for them
in that salt-box house
where stove pipes cracked
and stars winked
on the snow outside.
And that big, lazy man she married...
least of all I played for him
snoring on the settle
in the chimney corner,

a red face so peaceful
with the tea-pot waiting
and long rubbers limp and steaming
by the blushing stove.
And in all those years
of forget-me-not tunes,
she never guessed me
and my veil stayed down.

The Old Man And The Moon

We laughed at him then,
that old man so intent
on cleaning herring
with his finger nails.
We laughed at him
with silver scales over dirty fingers.
And we laughed
when he commented on the news:
"God'll never let them reach the moon."
We were boys remembering
back just a couple of catches
when we saw him smoke in silence,
watching his swaying nets drying
across the face of a rising moon.
He believed he saw a face
in the shine up there.
And we laughed then
as he talked to himself.

Now we are scattered men
remembering
back along a fish-spine row of years
to that time on the coast
of his belief
when the moving herring-schools
mooned in the long night tides
and tangled in the waiting nets
just yards below his quiet house
where he slept.

Figures From Ancestral Landscape

wind in the beams
    grandmother's hands
        kneading the bread

mackerel offshore
    south wind shadows
in the after-grass

tap-dancer at wedding
        turning to watch
  his shadow
    on the wall

leaving the house
of the newborn
  midwife
under winter moon

    pause
in old husband's tale
    the fool's laugh
    and the March wind

The Bear

Once in a long gone time
before any people came
and the island's trees
were spears of ice
against the frosty stars,
it came ashore
and used the land
as a stepping-stone
in polar-ice infinity.
The great tracks
in a wandering, cryptic chain
from shore to shore
were there for days and nights
before a snowfall
filled them in.
And dark spruce resounded
as rising surf
rolled ice offshore.

Years later, when a few people
lived here, there was once
a long winter famine
and the fish all gone,
and a grave-digger toiling
to get through frozen earth.
One day in this starvation spell
it came back again,
walking out of a white blizzard
like some clumsy giant
from the children's books,
walking towards the village guns,
bringing the famine to an end.

In another age, when only the old
remembered the hungry times,
it came ashore one day
from loose ice-pans
unlocking from the shoreline.
The people watched it cross the beach
on its way past flakes and stages
and low root-cellars.
With spears and guns

they tracked it to the tree-line.
Later, in a seaport town,
they charged admission, ten cents
to look at the carcass
propped up with ropes
against the wall of a merchant's shed.

Years later, with the island abandoned,
two boys returned one spring
to fish for trout
in the land of their ancestors,
and on a night
with pebbles clattering in landwash,
it returned, staggering,
brushing by their tent
on its way down river.
Next morning they found the body,
stiff under fly-buzzing
on the warm beach stones,
the head all swollen
where it had starved so long,
a tin can stuck
on the gangrene tongue.

Tonight, in a glow from television,
descendants of the island people
half listen to somebody
reading the late-night news,
reporting yet another
roaming near a town dump,
and government officials
on their way with the proper drug
to put it asleep,
cart it away somewhere
from civilized community.

Communion

In a faint memory of '52,
I can see the elders still
quaint like Gauguin's Breton folk,
or sometimes
creating the hell
of an old medieval masterpiece
where devils feed endlessly
on human flesh.
I can hear them too, arguing
and laughing on windy nights
in an aroma of cod
and kerosene,
when it was told
how the Devil
could take the form
of a great loon
laughing at us poor mortals
from somewhere
in the misty tide.
I can see a kitchen
and shadows crossing
on wallpaper.
The men are just back
from gunning
and, steaming on a supper table,
the carcass of a big loon
on a platter.

Evening, Bareneed, Conception Bay

A cold wind
creeps unmarked
through an old picket fence
and eats the salt-stained grass
already dead
on a skull of rock
above the bay
spilling itself
on the teeth
of kelp-ringed crags.

No birds in flight
on a slab of sky.
Beyond
across a bight
a slow mist hangs
in a cross
in a block of window light.

The Watcher

Once in Hemlock Cove
when a war
was somewhere
overseas
one man
was told
to check the lamps
each night.
And in the shadows
he walked
whistling to himself
secure in making sure
no German planes
far up in the mists
would ever know
a community waited.
But one night
he watched a young woman
dressing by a kerosene glow.
He watched
at her window
not bothering to tell her
of the "douting rules".
A half-naked woman
not worrying
about the news
from overseas
watched
by a man
who told himself
just this once
that one small light
would never matter.

The Naked Man

In a wet August day
with salt wind on berry leaves,
he loomed in fog
across a cape
and bog meadows slanting
down to an ocean's roar.
Around him dim cattle stood
still as rock piles
in the driftwood light.
Above him gulls screamed
down the dark tide
and gannets darted
in the herring shine.

I asked him to come
to guide me
down through marshes
where the pond was hidden.
But he had fences to mend
and cattle to tend
and a sure way for me
to find the pond myself.
His face was granite smiling
and offering a chair
by a cracking stove,
and a brown china mug
where kitchen saints
smiled down
through kettle steam.

Later, in half-gone morning,
I found his marker
to the pond,
his naked man
of piled weathered stones
and snarls
of dead juniper stump,
precarious
and leaning
on the tundra
wind.

Still later, returning
timidly in twilight,
I crept by the rock man
silently watching me now
wandering back
to my road-sign world
with small trout counted
in a plastic creel,
watching me
slipping on pathless moss,
groping
in metamorphic shadows,
in bog-sucking footsteps
away from those cryptic stones,
me, the most naked man of all.

The Widow And The Butcher Boy

"Paddy's comin' in a sleigh,"
She met him at the door,
A little house in a stony field
Engulfed by the ocean's roar.

A fisherman's widow in Torbay,
Behind her a fire bright,
And he a small boy with sausage to sell,
Afraid of the wild March night.

"Paddy's comin' in a sleigh,"
She smiled at his puzzled pause;
He wondered what her Paddy could do
Three months after Santa Claus.

She spoke of her sons, all overseas,
A row of dim frames on a wall,
A place with the saints all staring down,
Astir in a flickering pall.

"Paddy's comin' in a sleigh,"
She warned that he must be good;
Her round face shone in the warm spruce light
As she bent for a junk of wood.

She paid him from a coin purse
That hung like an old wet sock;
A fistful of buttons and candy
She drew from a fractured crock.

"Paddy's comin' in a sleigh,"
She chimed as he left the yard;
He chewed on a lump of peppermint
And swallowed very hard.

"Paddy's comin' in a sleigh,"
She echoed awhile in his head,
But he was too young and Protestant
To cherish what she said.

Peggy

They laughed at this simple girl,
she who was not like the others.
She who could be promised the stars
would let the boys do anything
for a coke and cigarette.
She shocked everybody
with her wild talk
of trees shedding blood
and devil's mark on haddock skin
and what she herself had heard
the animals say
in their dark stalls
on Christmas Eve,
and her visions of fairies
by an old wooden bridge
when the moon floated
on the tops of water stalks.
They made fun of the way
she scrawled pictures
of animals with wings,
and how she wept sometimes
at the clicking
of her aunt's knitting-needles
evenings when the sea called.

Finally the day came
when everybody left the cove
for good
and Peggy died
in a city somewhere.
But as the years passed,
those who had once laughed at her
began to talk
of going back
to a cove of bliss
with bobbing skiffs
in blessed light
and quaint little houses
with the good wives knitting.

47

Now there was a new way of believing
what ancestors had believed,
and a roundabout return
to elemental matters.
There was talk of exiled poets
scattered over cities and towns,
waiting out their lyric lives
for a chance to go back there
one more time.

Marsh

sun on whorl
   of pitcher plant
   and finger tip

scattered raindrops
   your fistful of berries
   pattering on tin

   mist on my face
white light
through wing of dragonfly

   heat ripples
moth dance
over beaver sticks

Vortex

Back home now
on that island
a window pane is broken
through which an ocean sighs
in a grey room
in a seeping dawn
and shadows
of wet sashes
and veins of glass
are netted
on an eastern wall.

I am there now
because I am away
from that room.

In a washed-granite stillness
in a spell of pebble light
a salt wind freshens again
and tunes departure's ode
through all sharp edges
of that window
and my vortex.

Perhaps a true homecoming
is really
a going-away.

Cape Shore Woman

I

(Before the Birds)

Waking before dawn,
Alone there in a big bed,
She waits for bird song.

In a north window:
Grey sky and dwarf spruce leaning
Back from sea strain.

Christ like a split cod
Across wallpaper shadows
And clock ticking.

Old things in her head:
Legend of the robin's breast
And ocean's roar.

II

(Getting Wood)

Going up the beach
Against the wind,
Gathering driftwood,
She stops
Suddenly
Still
Seeing
How close
The sandpiper
Will come.

III

(Shell Spell)

Sand spray
Stings
From the south west.
Turning
To make sure
She is alone
On the beach,
She tilts a shell
Against her ear,
Listening
For another sea.

IV

(A Tune)

Through kitchen window:
Dark notes
Of seabird
On silver sky
Turn white
Across cliffs
And sea caves.

From caverns
Behind her eyes:
The flutter
Of an old tune.
Tapping her foot
She tries
To coax it back.

V

(She Remembers)

When we were youngsters
back on the island,
I used to be mad after Joe Manning,
a fine strapping fellow
who could row a boat all day.
Once, at a dance out in Patrick's Cove,
I stood around all night
but he never even glanced my way.
God, it was tormenting
watching those wonderful arms
swing Kitty McGrath and Rosie O'Keefe
right off their feet.
Then, somewhere
between the jigs and the reels,
he left for Canada
before the war broke out
and he never came back
till 1982.

Life's a dance too,
I suppose...Ah, yes...
At a wedding in Placentia last year,
in loud music and the youngsters' fun,
he fumbled his way
across the hall
to dance with me.
He the pale scarecrow now
with the hair white
and face caved in,
and spindly arms
coaxing me off
from the wall
and my vision
of shoulder muscles
shiny and pulsing
like a stallion's
and wind-browned arms
and a ripple of oars
across a swell.

VI

(Trucks)

As fog creeps in
And spruce fade on the hills,
She stops to rest
Her water-bucket down
And watch four trucks
Pass up the winding road,
More antique dealers
From another town:

Dragged through the mist,
A motley mound of chairs,
Dark tables, trawl-tubs, clocks,
One gypsy chain,
Strange licence plates,
Ontario, Quebec,
The same to her,
One dusty, slipshod train.

Tonight she'll dream, perhaps,
She's young again
Out selling tubs
Of berries in the town;
Or, back from death,
Her husband baits a trawl
And curses on
The cold rain coming down.
Four sons fade away,
No time for fuss,
They're leaving for the mainland
On a bus.

VII

(Fireplace)

Tom Power's old place:
And the only thing standing,
A pile of flat stones.

Rocks from an island:
Chimney in the long grass swell.
Island now once more.

Fires in her head.
She strolls in sunset.
Sea breeze fans the land.

Warm foundation stones
Where the ghost stories came
When the nights were long

And Mary's kettle
Whistling against the frosty times,
Dancing on the grate.

Stage

No put put of the motor boat,
no waiting women placing boughs,
no children playing in the cliffs,
no cod-oil doors with painted moons,
no meadows green through caplin,
no sound-bone talk from tired men....

But one grey fish-stage
leaning seaward
from cold sloping rocks
below the meadows
of the unmown hay....

Top Of The World

Found this afternoon
at a flea-market:
an old rectangular map
called Top of the World,
just like the one we used
in rough, unready school days,
something free
from a mainland candy factory,
one big-as-life chocolate bar
adorning each corner.
And we in our frosty
hardtack times
were right up there,
bold print declaring it:
the big island of Newfoundland
in top of the world form.
But one day
in the bottom of winter,
a tattered group of us
were punished
for drawing our own
dragons of sorts,
a series of smutty pictures
across the wide, blank spaces
of open sea.
In spirit, we were not
so different really
from old, cautious cartographers
who sketched in sea monsters
as stays against emptiness,
or our methodical ancestors,
who were always in a hobble
about charting their ghosts,
those comforting spirits
so necessary in barren spots
between communities.

A Consecration

Luke remembered
their last days on the island
gathering what was
to be taken
as young gulls swayed
above the sun-grazed swell
and a lingering mist
ghosted in the garden gleam.
And he remembered
the clergyman telling them
to burn all the boards
from the dismantled church
because such wood was consecrated.
But next day Luke's brother came
in a big white skiff
and took the wood away
to build a house.
And as the months passed
Luke was uneasy
about the anointed wood
until the morning
when he heard the meek cry
of his brother's firstborn
within the sanctuary
of the new walls
as dawn stroked window glass
and kettle mist ascended
to the sturdy beams.

In A Small Cove

Sheer cliffs in sea-song.
And seeking in close spring fog,
Sheep above roof tops.

The French Shore Man

Seems I can mind them
myself,
the French
along our coast,
and poor father
and his father before him
talking about the wonderful bread
those foreigners made
in beach-rock ovens
in the summertime.
That was well back
in the rowdy days
when they thought
this shore
belonged to them.
Sometimes they seemed pretty human
all the same,
giving you one
of their queer loaves
to go with your fish
when you crossed paths
on the water,
even though you were English
with wife and youngsters
on the shore.
It must have been hard
for them to accept defeat
and leave the coves
where they cured their cod.
I remember
poor grandfather grinning,
claiming he broke bread
with them one time
somewhere off the Grey Islands...

On raw days now
when the wind is in
and the sand taps
my window pane,
I can close my eyes
and see them
moving
in the landwash still...
Dreamy foolishness, I suppose,
for me with sixty summers notched.

But one day
six years ago,
I was digging a hole
to put the bark-pot on,
when all of a sudden,
my pick struck Frenchmen's bones.
Seems there were two of them
laid out there.
One had no teeth at all;
that devil yawned at everything.
The other had all his ivory,
no mistake about that,
and when I laid his skull
on a rock,
he seemed to stare
out over the water,
grinning at it all.

Bonfire Night

Quick stray snowflakes
and a squall
up from Baccalieu
through the dogberry trees.

The shouts
of youngsters.
A doll
on a long dark stick
swings
against the night.

On billows
of collapsing
cod-oil drums
the bottomless dory
lifts
    one
        last
           time.

The Ballad Of Flora

The widow, Flora Livingstone,
Was lonely in her bed,
With lots of money put away,
Poor husband Sam was dead.

A strapping lad named Billy King
Who kept her cattle fed,
Was lusting for her seaside fields
With voices in his head:

"You're thirty now, she's sixty-odd;
She's picked you as the one;
Present her with a wedding-ring,
She wants a man, my son!"

They married in the month of May,
The fog released the sun,
And a fiddler from far away
Led off the village fun.

Young Billy King was gloating now,
He'd put up with her bed,
He owned the cattle on the hills,
He saw good times ahead.

The warm wind darted in the hay,
A summer's silver thread;
In lobster-crawl and snipe-bawl time,
A worm stirred in his head:

"She'll grow more feeble with the fall,
Her time cannot be long;
You'll still be spry when she is dead,
Your limbs are young and strong!"

But Flora flourished with the years,
While Billy's hair turned gray;
The sea wind darted to his bones
When fog rolled on the bay.

Something of fey in Flora's face,
An old man in her bed
A-snoring in the snipe-bawl time;
A worm stirred in her head:

"He'll grow more feeble with the fall,
His time cannot be long;
You'll still be spry when he is dead;
Your roots run deep and strong!"

In Picasso's "Madman"

Somehow, in Picasso's "Madman",
I can see the four of them:

Uncle Henry Gaunt
just back from the Labrador,
bent over Aunt Carrie's grave,
crying in his big, cupped hands,
then stopping suddenly
to peer through knotty fingers
at aspen leaves
trembling on a white sky.

And my tired grandfather,
daydreaming in the landwash,
gazing through a web of caplin mesh
strung on his splayed fingers
in a moment
when he did not see me
watching him.

And poor Jenny Drake,
the war-bride
knitting by a kitchen window,
ignoring her baby's crying,
staring through the yarn-lines
in her thin fingers,
talking again of cowslip fields
and heather-slopes
across the sea.

And the retarded boy
who lived one time in Rampike Arm,
lying hidden under cherry-limbs,
talking to his contorted hands,
laughing excitedly
to himself
each time mosquitoes clustered
for his blood...

...Something of four people
I knew one time,
now glimmering
in Picasso's tattered "Madman"
forever fascinated
with those invisible skeins
all tangled
in his scrawny hands.

Haiku(1)

dawn flecks
in lees
of buttercup

doryman
lifts herring-net
and morning moon

Haiku (2)

sunlight on the wing
    seagull ascending
        over chapel ruins

somewhere
from white cloud
    a cry of tickle-ace

Haiku (3)

cliff-top tuckamore
     goat hooves ringing
     on a shale sky

mushroom cloud
    man against sky
   with hay on his back

Haiku (4)

after northeaster
    spreading seaweed
on her flower bed

                on rain-washed wall
                    the shadow of a pitch-fork
                    and afternoon sun

Haiku (5)

lying in alders
waiting for loon's cry
to take shape

water strider
stirring clockwise
on the moon

On Cuslett Brook (1979)

Just the three of us fishing there
in the purl of an August afternoon:

On my left, upstream,
through leaf filigree,
caught in a glint
of mote-dancing sunlight,
my young son
so Icarian in summer energy,
spin-casting metal
into pools of sky.

On my right, downstream,
my father,
eternal worm-and-bobber man,
stirring from a partial Buddha stance,
bear-like in beach rock haze,
shambling around
the last pool
before the sea.

I dream Silver Doctor
and siren tug
on double-tapered line.
I have the middle water
all to myself
and a line or two
of old Heraclitus
in my head:
something about our never being
able to ascend the same brook twice.

Edwardians (Old Photograph)

For them it is always Sunday afternoon:
six couples in the shade of a tree,
lounging in an English meadow.

They are blurred now:
sepia smokers in straw hats
lolling among wine bottles,
cake-baskets, clover.

They stare out at us:
lotus creatures, insolent somehow
in languid pose,
smug, sprawling, laid-back,
locked there in weekend.

Behind them, over daisy-dotted trench,
a jacket swings carelessly
on a strand of wire
dividing the property,

winding, coiling towards the Channel
perhaps, one inconspicuous,
barbed, metallic cord,
not really symbolic
in this landscape yet.

Back Road

As I walk by the house tonight
I am wondering
about Walt, Fred, Tom,
Doug, Steve, and Sam.
They have disappeared somewhere
on the mainland,
have not been back home
since they left in the sixties
one by one.
I wonder also about Geraldine
who was glad that summer
to cross the gulf
and live with an aunt
in Cape Breton for good,
and young Madaline
who perished
on the streets of Vancouver.

I find myself recalling
how short childhood was
in a past with not much
time for play.
I see them always
in hand-me-downs,
tending rocky meadows
and damp potato drills,
and cod to be cured
from rough water
four miles away,
the curse of the puritan
pervading everything.

The parents are alone tonight,
keeping the big two-story house
as best they can.
Samuel is seventy,
Nora is sixty-nine.
The lawn is tidy
with their own toys now:

Creatures from the comic strips
crouch everywhere.
Samuel just polished
a plywood Garfield yesterday.
Last week he removed the moons,
painting circus ponies
on barn and cellar doors.
And Nora, this Halloween,
kept one grinning lantern
lit up in a window
all night.

The Veteran (1)

I'll not forget that foreign scene,
and I just a frightened boy:
He tarried there in my rifle-sight,
So tall on the clearing sky.

I struggled to pull the trigger then,
For, just beyond his head,
Was a flash of something close to home,
Across those fields of the dead:

A wink of sea between two hills,
A gull's turn on the sky,
I stopped and put my rifle down
And let my man pass by.

The Veteran (2)

"Take what you can
From those you kill",
Our commander let us know;
"A watch, a chain, or anything,
whatever you can stow."

I didn't heed him at the time,
I didn't want their gold,
But one day on a gory field
When wind was whipping cold,
I snatched a locket from the neck
Of a German boy I'd shot;
He was sprawled face down
In a muddy pool
And blood was spilling hot.
The locket had a golden heart
With two smiling women inside;
One had to be his mother,
The other one, his bride.

And there in cold rain
And the raven's croak,
I flung that keepsake away,
A locket like the one I wore
For Mary and Mother that day.

Wild Geese

They are passing by, low again,
as they did five summers ago,
their wing beat stirring
the yellow afternoon
of sky and clear pond waters
back through pliant mounds of turf
warm above wave-lilt
over mossy stones.

This was always
my own fishing place
until one day five summers ago
I met him there,
a bent man berry-picking
who said he always thought
this was his secret pond,
but never mind...
I could have it now
as his legs were not
what they used to be.
We sat eating berries
where the brook departed,
watching two wild geese
rise slowly from the lily-pads,
their shadows grazing us
as they turned westward
to fade over distant rampikes.

Today I am watching
the two great birds again
rise up as if a bell
were sounding somewhere
in the partridge berry hills.
They swing westward
where sky meets marsh leaves,
their shadows almost
touching me.

Sandpiper

It hopped
across the pool-streaked sand
as the tide was coming in,
with legs like straws
that would not bend,
and a low, piping call
on the rising wind.

It skipped
along the mussel-beds
as the sun dropped
from the sky,
and faded somewhere
in the surf
with a lonely, twittering cry.

If Sonnets Were In Fashion

If sonnets were in fashion,
I think I would try one
about a dog I heard
barking one time
in a taped poetry reading
by Robert Frost.
The imagery would be geological
and the old man of fire and ice,
plain diction, the gravel voice
could have the octave
all to himself,
free to be crafty
yet seeming so undesigning
within the confines
of iambic walls,
his presentation glacial, powerful,
moving on the slow import
of its melting....
And then, intruding into line eight,
in a tree-at-my-window pause,
that audible fossil,
just for a couple of seconds,
a dog barking faintly somewhere.

The creature would have the sestet
all to itself,
so perfectly autonomous out there
in pussy-willow swamp
and prime New England sunshine,
casually scanning its territory,
cocking its leg
against the world perhaps,
its primitive spondee
lingering and wonderful.
Oblivious to any
iamb or anapest,
it would just be
its own wild poetry,
a summons
from the wordless places
once again.

"Struggle Into Light": a Poem To John Clare

"A struggle into light,"
was what you called it,
your flash into a fame of sorts
in a world
where rustic bards like yourself
were going out of fashion.
Yours was a sun-on-a-petal spell,
a dart of robin-red,
quick trout-dapple
in the dawn.

I can picture you too
glowing for awhile
in old London town,
stomping big country boots
along the cobblestones,
a bit of a Bobby Burns
in your homespun jacket,
your love of ale,
and twinkle for the lasses.

When you arrived back home,
trying to find poems
in the fields again,
there were curious souls
always coming by in carriages
to see what a peasant poet,
so unlettered and all,
could be doing
in his element.

It must have been weary, John,
with fields to be tilled
and babies to be fed.
One time you called it
"wearing into sunshine"
when those literary folk
dropped by and called you
from your labours.
And you complained too
how you were promised books
and all kinds of patronage
before they dropped their heads
in smug, "Good morning attitudes."

Years later, in your final fading,
did you expect very much
when they shipped your corpse home
from Northampton Asylum in 1864?
Could you believe that nobody,
not even one of your own,
would come to receive you?
Could you ever see
your remains
being waked in the shadows
of a village pub?

And, as for your last request,
when you asked for burial
on the north side
of the churchyard,
right in middle ground,
where sun could linger
on your grave,
did you expect
that they would grant you
middle ground?

Were you surprised, John,
when they moved you south
to the coldest side
where the sun hardly lingers
at all?
Were you somehow
expecting it
when they set you down
in cold clay
where the shadow
of a chancel
falls?

Alders

Last night I dreamed
they were bringing the world
back,
verdant tongues calling out
to a sun again;
but we were no longer
a part of it.
There had been great snows,
grey rock, and serrated forms
against a sky.
Millions of what we used to
call years had passed
before that
spear of green
between two stones,
that thrust of arrowhead.
Always apprehensive
of their coming,
we had massacred
in the name of clearing,
we who had whittled
small music sometimes
from their supple bones.

Fearful of advance scout,
of any forerunner
of wilderness,
we had always killed
messengers.

Methodists

It is a Sabbath evening
in Edwardian Newfoundland
and the house is being readied
for my great grandfather's passing:

a few last words to a semi-circle
of souls around his bed;
the murmured consolation of Scriptures;
the adjusting of big feather pillows
around his head;
in a corner, a woman's whispering,
re-creating the strange white bird
against a window yesterday.

Outside in a dim hallway
more whispering,
a solemn shaking of heads
recalling his meticulous clearing
of the droke two days ago:
too much for one man
with axe and mattock, they said.

His wife seeks out his prayer-book,
his Orangeman's sash,
his good suit all pressed,
put away systematically
for the proper occasion.

Now only one thing remains:
somebody must go out
and knock on the door
of the Methodist church,
ask them to keep the noise down
so a man can die peacefully
just up the road.

Bitch

She appeared in the season of small leaves,
stopping to beg
outside our gate one day.
I was seven that summer in caplin time,
and she had been foraging
along the beach,
scrawny, black and white intruder,
little lone ranger
among the gulls and big crows
who watched her suspiciously.
I had been warned
to stay away from her;
dogs were useless anyway,
my father said.
Besides, she was almost blind
and flies droned around
the damp mask of her eyes.
But I still swear she saw
me clearly that day, watching her
in the slow dust of afternoon;
our communion
crossing centuries somehow,
before I tossed a crust of bread to her
and ran.

Years later I found her bones
in boggy woods beyond our cove,
no attitude of begging
in them anymore:

and up from an eye socket,
the pronged genesis
of an aspen tree.

Today, so many years later,
in a strange city,
in an arid valley
between apartment buildings,
I hear wind in an aspen tree:

that silver-green clicking of dry bones,
all those little dry bones
reassembling.

Calling The Children

Somewhere at a lane's end,
through nettles pinned on boggy twilight,
and the frame of a rusting car
upside down in cherry blossoms,
the children are barking
bare-footed in puddle mud.
And mothers are peeping
through metal frames of windows and doors
and calling "bedtime", "Billy",
"Jane" and such.
The fathers who used to
swim in that almost-gone puddle,
are sleeping in front of television sets.
The children do not hear
their mothers' voices;
they have sharpened spears
from fingers of the cherry limbs
to kill all the tadpoles.
And now in the going sun
the pool is muddy blood.
They will take their own time
coming home this evening
carrying sweet blossoms
for their mothers' hair.

Daedalus

Alone on the beach this morning
I catch myself
blaming the gods again
for this poised gull
against the sky,
mocking me now
as they did once
at my son's funeral
when a partridge laughed
from somewhere
in the grove.
I dream that day back
with gentle sea swell,
goats, green island,
the lip of a grave,
and sorrow planting me
like some tree
twisted
in sea wind.

On morning wings
across the sun
he comes before me,
there at the seabird's core,
my son,
the slave-girl's child,
that shadowy
all-too-human form,
five-pointed man
inside translucent feather.
Cruel are those gods
who coax
with sunshine!

Now I am forced
to see him
falling
once more,
clawing
the air
so far
beyond

my pleading.
And as he goes
by me,
one last
glimpse
of the slave
girl
free somehow
in frightened
contours
of his face.
And the mesmerizing
space
of it all,
the small flag
of a foot
disappearing
into the shimmer
of the herring
shoals.

And far away,
as if they know
about it already,
waiting, nodding,
placed there
for my returning,
sinewy, sunburned men,
like a chorus
of cormorants,
picking their snarled nets
along a sea-wall,
voicing their platitudes
against all heedless youth;
the mesh of an old hubris
closing in again.

Daedalus At Garden Wall

On the day when I finished this wall,
he was only five or so,
playing with clam shells
in the landwash below me.
I was anxious that morning,
fearful that he might wander off,
go following goat-paths up the cliffs,
slip away somewhere
into the kelpy murmur.
So I called him back,
kept him close, talked to him,
until the work was completed.
And then, into my last patch of cement,
while it was still wet and pliable,
I pressed his small hand.

Today I find myself stepping back
to admire the mark,
the short fingers splayed
like rays of sun
in a child's drawing.
The hand is fading now,
edges crumbling as I stroke it.

Back on that day
I was confident craftsman,
one stoical
about what the rain's chisel,
the sea-wind's hammer could do.

Today, alone in the wall's lee,
I am shocked
by the corrosive power
in a sparrow's song,
a blade of leaf,
a snail's crawl,
a shadow of scudding cloud.

Seabird

The oil-soaked carcass,
    seaweed ganglia,
    broken glass,
  in a whirl of sand.

Under shell crust,
  that fearful something
    from the tar,
  the center holding.

Alone in front of it,
    I daydream.
  In my own crude circle,
  thumb meeting index finger,
    I conjure phoenix.
    Matting the dark form,
    I seek relief
    in raised design
    of cameo.

But from noon's shimmer
  over fly-blown stones,
the desert's warning

  that art will not be
    sanctuary

  this time.

Salmon

Once in a mind-over-matter spell,
    lost epoch of prime communion,
she was always mystical,
        wise prophetic creature,
        proficient ring-bearer,
        eternal battler,
    emblem of folk heroes,
    patron saints and kings,
her flesh forbidden
        to all those outside
        sovereign estate.

This morning in low, rusty water,
    she was spotted,
tallied by federal government officials
        at a river mouth,
        entered in a record-book
        as the first fish
        for August 13, 1991,
and let in through a gate.

Tonight, in a shrinking tributary,
    under alders
    and cold stars,
    she will gasp
    in the arms
    of a poacher's son.

Hide And Seek

It was an August evening,
just after supper, in 1949,
when six of us met
for hide-and-seek
in the shadow of Uncle John's
slaughter-house,
"the shammel" we called it.
Freddy Smith lined us up
and started counting:

"Eenie, meenie, miney, mo..."

Marie was the first to go
and she with the swinging pig-tails
went wraith-like
laughing across an oat field.
On the next tally,
Skinny Charley followed her,
loping like a hound dog.
Soon Judy and panting Alice
went tumbling after.
I was left with Freddy
eager to count himself out
and call me "It".
His finger, like a lance,
tapped time on my chest
and the rhyme raced on,
one mad cacophony.

"It's not fair," I called
as he raced away
across the stubble.
I was alone
near the blood-tub.
A quarter moon
sickled on the sky.

"Eenie, meenie..."
I counted on the clapboards
waiting for them to call.
The blood of last week's lamb
came up on honeysuckle.
I waited..."miney, mo..."
but all was quiet.

And then the years passed
and I heard from Marie again.
Seems she'd married an American
much against her father's wishes
and when she telephoned, in 1960,
crying from somewhere down in Alabama,
the old man wouldn't
even come to the phone.
Skinny Charley bled to death
in Viet Nam,
just after he'd sent his brother
a big beer-mug
shaped from one of the shells.
In 1978, I found Judy,
cosy in a Boston accent
and vowing she would never
come home again.
Alice and Freddy crossed paths
and got married
somewhere in Ontario.
Last year, at the conclusion
of a poetry reading in Labrador,
their eldest son
came up from the back
to say how small the world was
and wish me well.

Lightning Source UK Ltd.
Milton Keynes UK
UKOW04f1909250315

248537UK00001B/198/P